MW00639361

Testimony of Gloria Polo

Standing Before God:
The Judgment

By Martín Zavala

Information and how to place an order:

Mission 2000
P.O. BOX 51986
PHOENIX, AZ 85076
Tel. (480) 785-0310

Our website:

www.anewevangelization.com

"Books That Change Lives"

Editing: *Martín Zavala*
Art directing: *Martín Zavala*
Designing: *Martín Zavala*

Dedication:

This book is dedicated to my beautiful family. To my wife Silvia and my children, Louis, Elsa and Andres.

Martín Zavala

Notice

Our intention when sharing this Book is not to confirm its supernatural character but to recommend it for it's great spiritual benefit.

Publisher Mission 2000

"*The so-called - private - revelations do not belong to the deposit of faith. It is not their role to - improve - or - complete - Christ's definitive Revelation, but to help live more fully by it in a certain period of history.*"

Catechism of the Catholic Church No. 67

CONTENT

Introduction

I am not bad
My judgment... and I discovered who I truly was
At a moment, they opened "the book of life"
The reality of my sin
I help Satan throw others into hell using my words

But my life was filthy with sin
I used to think that I was a powerful woman but I was
lost in sin
What spiritual treasures do you bring
I was Catholic in my own way
I couldn't deny myself the truth
Dad had forgotten the most important thing

I supported Satan with the blood of abortion
I began to see abortion as a good option
The beast tells us that the bad is good, and we believe it
I thought I wasn't an adulterer, but I was wrong again
I did not have an abortion, but I recommended it
as a good option

Introduction

A couple of days ago we were on a mission in San Diego, California when they recommended that we see a video of the Testimony of Dr. Gloria Polo. They informed me that it was something truly unbelievable because she had been struck by lightning during a storm which caused her and her nephew's death. After the lightning struck, she found herself in a special place where God judged her and then allowed her to come back to tell her spiritual story.

Personally, I had heard of occasions that were similar, but I didn't fully understand them. However when we were on break, I couldn't help but notice the DVD on the table. I started watching it and quickly found myself captivated by the story that Gloria was telling. She wasn't preaching, she wasn't an unbelievable public speaker, nor was it a sensational or emotional message,; yet, I couldn't stop watching it.

It was the testimony of somebody who was 100% sure of what she was saying as she shared the experience of returning from the dead. And I realized as I listened to her story that everything she was saying fit perfectly into Catholic doctrine. It was like she had a doctorate in theology but was speaking in simple words. It was as though she was speaking in a clear and profound language typical of the mystics.

When I finished the video, something happened to me, something that had happened to thousands of other people. I quickly said to myself "I need to go to confession, right now." Immediately after watching the DVD, it was impossible for us to not question ourselves and want to start over again to be better people.

In fact, someone called me a couple of days ago, soliciting help because she had seen the video of Dr. Gloria Polo and felt that she had to change her life. She told me that she was an alcoholic and an adulterer among other things, but now the testimony of Gloria had convinced her to convert to Jesus Christ.

That is why **Mision 2000** decided to contact Gloria and invite her to Arizona to record her testimony with a professional recording crew. The new DVD that we made is called "My Judgment before God." If you have not seen it, I recommend that you purchase it at www.gloriapolo.us

As time passed, we found that a lot of people wanted the testimony of Gloria Polo in book form and that is why you are holding this special edition in your hands.

Another great blessing of reading this book is that you will be able to learn about the historic and biblical sense of the Judgment, Purgatory, Heaven, and of Hell; which are topics that are key in the testimony of Gloria. Surely the extra chapter dealing with these topics that has been included in this testimony will strengthen you in the Catholic faith and help you answer the atheists and the fundamentalist evangelicals that question these teachings.

Besides, we have included some of the thousands of testimonies from people who have heard the message of Gloria and have been blessed by it. We hope this message will be a blessing to you as well.

As if that weren't enough, at the end of the book, we have added a chapter with prayers for the souls in purgatory, due to the fact that after reading this testimony, some of you might feel the need to pray for your lost loved ones.

For all of the reasons above I strongly recommended this book. I am 100% convinced that when you are done reading, you will decide to advance in Holiness on your walk with Christ.

I hope that you read this to the greater glory of God and for your spiritual well-being.

Your friend and brother in Christ, Martin Zavala

Phoenix, Arizona 2014

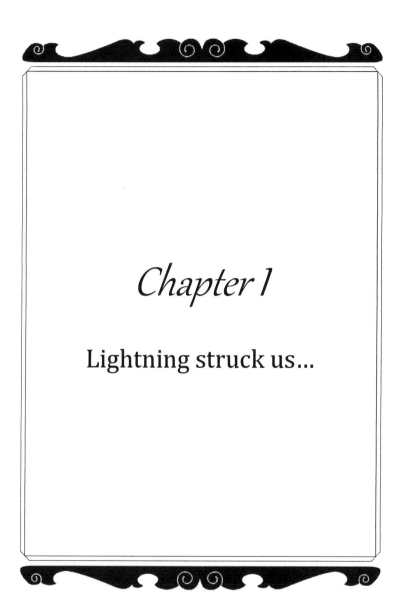

Chapter 1

Lightning struck us...

A Lightning bolt struck us...

and a beautiful tunnel appeared

Brothers and sisters, I truly thank God, the Father, for being able to be here with you sharing this beautiful gift that I received from the Lord on May 5th, 1995. I was at the National University that day. It was on a Friday around 4:30, I was with my husband and nephew. My nephew and I were doing a specialization in orthodontics. It began to rain, we had to go to the Dentistry Faculty. While we were on our way... lightning struck us.

You have no idea how impressive that was. There was a giant tree next to us and it was completely charred. There was a hole left on the ground where the lightning fell. We were by the foot of the tree, the lightning entered through my nephew's heart and exited through his foot. His flesh was not burnt, nor his body. Only two burns were left on him. One was on his heart, the image of the Child Jesus was left, from a chain he was wearing. There was also a small hole in his foot where the lightning exited.

He and I went into cardiac arrest immediately, without any vital signs. The difference was my nephew did not come back when the doctors tried to revive him; he was barely twenty-three when he went into the presence of our Lord.

As for me, brothers and sisters, you cannot imagine the gift of God it is, that you can even see me standing up. It was horrible when the lightning entered my arm. It charred my whole arm, and removed all the flesh from my fingers.

I used to be very vain and always showed cleavage. I played a lot of sports and did a lot of aerobics and weight training, but the lightning charred my breasts and removed all the flesh; especially the left breast in which almost all of it was gone and half of the right breast. All the flesh on my stomach, of my abs was gone. My legs were as a pair of coals and were without flesh, the bone was left bare.

My liver was burnt, my lungs seriously suffered as well as my ovaries because the electricity not only burns outside but inside as well.

I was using an intrauterine device (IUD) called copper T for contraception. Do you know what the doctors said about my ovaries? The doctors explained it to me using these words, "Your ovaries and your tubes are like raisins, completely burnt."

Just like my nephew, I had gone into cardiac arrest, but the difference was that our Lord allowed me to return. When we stopped being electrically charged, they took us to the infirmary and the doctors performed CPR.

They took a while to pick us up because we had so much electricity running through us; there was a lot of water and it was full of electricity.

My husband was very close to us but he did not get burnt. However, he was left unconscious with some electricity; he was very, very beaten by the blow of the electricity, just as we were.

He brought me back

While they were performing the resuscitation, my husband stayed for the removal of my nephew's body. They took me to the Samaritan's hospital and quickly performed a surgery to clean all my burnt tissue.

I was seriously ill during the surgery, and had a second cardiac arrest. When I was having that second cardiac arrest, the doctors revived me. They incubated me and went to tell my family, "look, there is nothing we can do for her, she is so burnt that we cannot begin to evaluate how many more burns she has in her interior; that is why we advise not to connect her to an intensive care unit, because there is no quality of life for her."

Imagine, I was a defender of euthanasia; I was a promoter of the famous "dignified" death. Thank God I could not choose, because I was unconscious, or I would have chosen to die with "dignity". Do you know where I would be right now, brothers and sisters? In Hell. But thanks be to God my family chose for me. I lasted three days in a coma, seriously ill and dying. They became more ill each day because my kidneys were not able to filter out liquids. My lungs were totally full of water, I had a pulmonary edema, a giant pleural effusion and my heart was just plain weak.

Do you know what the Lord allowed? When I arrived at that moment of the agony of death, when I was already agonizing, and from the very door of death *He brought me back*. When He brought me back, to the surprise of the doctors and my family, my kidneys and lungs immediately began to work-just like that. They were able to take the respirator off the next day.

We must amputate the two legs
They took me to the Samaritan's hospital, to the burn unit, where I lived a very painful period of my life in which they scraped my burnt tissue every day. That process lasted a month and a half as they cleared my tissue daily. But my legs, could not feel anything.

I was devastated when the doctors said, "we must amputate your legs, because they do not respond, there is no circulation and we cannot allow the necrosis of the legs to affect the rest of your body." I used to spend my time doing aerobics and was always dancing, I would always go out. I loved dancing and now they are telling me that they want to cut off my legs!

I came from a very poor family and I tried to leave that poor life, to work hard and study hard. Those were my values. *I thought that the sole purpose of life was to come to the world to make money* however you could. To work hard, to study hard and to make money.

When they were going to cut off my legs, I realized that money is not good for anything because money cannot buy a new pair of legs and I begged God our Lord to leave me my legs, and then a great miracle happened.("By His stripes we have been healed" Is 53) He allowed me to keep my legs as you can see, although one leg is a bit lame because it was so burnt that my foot was slumped.

Our Lord did not heal it completely but left it a bit lame. Now I must use rubber shoes or I will experience great pain. It is the one thing that remains.

I was left without breasts and part of my side kept bleeding for a long time and the Lord allowed that pain for a year and a half. After a year and a half, in blessing, I had got up without breasts and went to bathe and had breasts! The Lord replaced them in one night, He had formed my breasts and replaced them. I did not have breasts, all the flesh had fallen and only the nipples were left. That part of my side also filled, the one that bled for a long time. I also did not have a menstrual cycle and they told me, "you will never have children because your ovaries were charred."

Then for the glory of God, the Lord replaced my breasts and filled all this flesh because **I was pregnant**. I had a daughter, her name is Maria José, today my girl is nine years old. At great speed are great miracles.

My first great physical miracle from our Lord was to survive so long in cardiac arrest without oxygen in my brain and to not lose my neural stability. I could have been left a vegetable, but *God had other plans for me brothers and sisters*.

I saw it all at the same time, as if the Lord had lent me His eyes

It is the most beautiful and most wonderful thing, forgive me because there are no human words to make you understand and to describe this moment.

When that lightning hit me, I immediately entered an indescribable light, a love, peace, and an infinite joy. Words cannot come close to describing it; I was free of time and space. I saw an immense light at the end like a beautiful sun beating.

I saw all men and women, everybody at the same time as if the Lord had lent me His eyes and I could see all of humanity in an instant; but not as I used to see, because my sight was one of a pagan woman, who looked at people in church and said "she is well dressed, she is fat, she is skinny." Now when I saw all the people, I saw their interior not just their exterior, their thoughts, their feelings, and their sins.

Do you know what impacted me the most? *To see that sin is alive*, it hit me hard to see sin. They are impure spirits, one says that I am a liar, I hate, I am adulterous, and I am an alcoholic. One thinks that all of that evil remains outside, well no brothers and sisters, when one sins, that enters to live within you and sin opens the door to another sin and another vice.

When I saw all of humanity in an instant, I felt an infinite pain seeing how we have lost love, compassion, kindness, and mercy. How all those impure spirits live inside people and how those poor people are enslaved

18

within, with those things inside. I felt such pity, I embraced the people, I embraced everyone, I wanted people to feel the love that was inundating me.

Nobody felt me, the only one that felt when I was embracing her was my daughter, the oldest one, who today is in the Convent, she was nine then, when I see her, I embraced her and she felt me; she turned around to look at me but was scared because she didn't see me.

My husband shouted: Gloria don't be a coward! Gloria, come back!

I went up, going up into an infinite love. The more I went up, the more love flooded over me. When I was approaching I saw that the light that beats is the Heart of Jesus, and how beautiful was that beating Heart. I saw two beautiful trees and a lovely lake; a living water, a love that is alive in the end. A lovely garden, a beautiful lake.

I realized that the Heart was wounded and that the wound was the entrance to that garden. I wanted to enter quickly, I was in that joy when I heard the voice of my husband, my husband shouted and said to me, "Gloria, please do not go. Gloria, come back. The children, Gloria, the children."

At that moment, my ascent stopped and I saw him bleeding and *I saw him crying*. Brothers and sisters, how great is the Sacrament of marriage, how great; imagine that when he calls me and shouts; he attracts my attention, after I am enjoying the love of God. Do you know what? Shamefully brothers and sisters, I looked at him not because I loved him, but because of the power of the sacrament.

I tell you the truth, at that moment, my marriage was at the worst moment of its life. Regrettably a feminist(me) gets married. I was a feminist woman, the defender of women; I used to say the woman does not have to be subdued, the woman must stop being stupid, the time of our mothers, who tolerated their husbands when they did whatever they wanted, those men who were vulgar, rude, alcoholics, and dogs, that time is over; that was my motto.

I would say no! If the woman had an unfaithful man, let her get even or leave him and learn to work, not depend on those hideous ones. That was my motto, I would not tolerate it. I married a chauvinist male, dominant and alcoholic. So, you can imagine the marriage; we had a war to death from the beginning.

We committed a very great error, **to kill the love**, and do you know what it was? To begin to insult each other, hurt each other with words. And we came to the point in our marriage that whenever we saw each other it was to see who could hurt the other more and who could offend more. He talked about my body and sometimes said that I was fat or that I was losing my waist and I would say "you are not a man, you are good for nothing."

Imagine, me messing with him for the mere act of hurting him and him hurting me. Every time we saw each other we hurt each other. Our poor children, we had two, in the middle of that war.

You should've seen us. When my daughter sat down to eat lunch with us on Sundays that is when she saw us. She would always spill her drink, it spilled out of the panic she had for her father and I, to see at what time we began the war, what a pity, but we didn't care about the children, we cared about who won that battle.

I begin to see something horrible

I came to that point, where my husband is crying; I stare at him, didn't he hate me so much then? Now he is crying for me not to leave. When I was staring at him I was sent back, I did not want to go back, but I had no freedom and I was sent back to find my body without life.

I saw my body without life and I saw the doctors bringing me out of cardiac arrest. I arrived and put my feet on my forehead, when I put my feet on my head I felt a yank as if they were pulling me. I was sucked into my body with violence and I jumped in my body, you can imagine, brothers and sisters, the pain of my burnt body.

Imagine the pain to breathe as if I was burnt on the inside and the shocking pain to swallow saliva. The pain to my vanity, how much money I spent and how much hunger I tolerated to keep my body in great shape as best as I could; I took care of it all my life and in an instant I had no body, it was charred.

When they took me to the Samaritan Hospital, I had a second experience; do you know where the first one was? Remember me, brothers and sisters, when you are there. When we all die, our Lord embraces us and brings us to His Heart and shows us how great the love that He has for us is. This God that loves us so much, the greatest sign of His love which is this Cross, the Sacrifice of love. Yet, there is another sign of love that our Lord Jesus has for us.

He loves us so much that He respects man's freedom. *If someone in this life has lived here according to the devil*, hurting others, mistreating people, humiliating them, mistreating his wife, his children, destroying all who approach him, hating, lying, and murdering; then who is their father?

That is easy, he that one has chosen as father. The Lord who respects so much the freedom of the person, if a person has lived here on earth without God, he is going to be without God in eternity. That was what happened when the Lord withdrew me from His Heart and delivered me to the father of lies. What happened?

When I had that second cardiac arrest, I began to see people start coming out of the walls of the operating room, seemingly ordinary but with an evil glance of hatred and with horror.

Imagine brothers and sisters, the horror when one realizes that sin is not free, that sin has its wage. The wage of sin was me, the one who had accepted it. When I saw that sin came to pick me up, you cannot imagine the horror that I felt. I ran away, I fled.

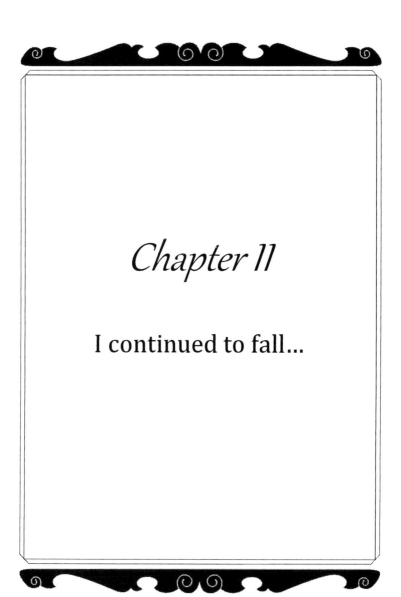

Chapter 11

I continued to fall...

I continued to fall ...

And I screamed desperately, "let me out!"

When I went through the wall of the operating room, I leaped into the dark and I entered a bunch of cells like jails, like honeycombs. There were thousands and thousands of people there. In the beginning, there was a lot of light and as I was going down, the light was fading away.

Where I was, there was a great light. I saw the people in those jails with dresses like the sun, shining like a fire, white like a sun, and beautiful. I saw my mother who had already passed away, there in those cells. She was so beautiful, her clothes were beautiful, and white as a snow.

I realized something. Do you know why I always say I realized? When I lost my flesh, my flesh was there without life. My understanding was a poor mental process, but now I had wisdom about everything, a knowledge. That's why I knew, without anyone telling me anything, when I saw them dressed like the sun. I realized how beautiful Eucharistic souls are.

Each time a person goes and receives our Lord, Sacramental Jesus in the Eucharist, their soul as if full of holes is dressed by the Flesh of the Lamb of God, by the Flesh of Jesus and within them the Blood of Jesus begins to circulate. They are beautiful, especially the souls that go to the Blessed Sacrament of the Altar, they are most beautiful, that is why they beautifully shine so bright.

I could not remain with them because I continued to fall. When I was falling they were becoming more and more deformed, the people with living darkness moving within them. When I was much lower, it smelled horrible and I realized that the one who smelled the worst was me. For the first time, I saw myself interiorly.

I was a 'catholic by default'
When I saw myself interiorly, I screamed like crazy, because I realized how frightful a soul without confession is. I had all those sins inside that screamed, that moved, that laughed. It seemed like a living hell, just as my mother seemed like a sun, I seemed like a deformed beast.

The sin had deformed me, that is why I ended up being a feminist, a defender of women. Imagine, do you know who Gloria Polo was? A "light", "diet" Catholic. Everything in my life was diet; among those, Catholicism. Do you know who are the Diet Catholics? The ones that barely goes to Mass on Sunday, if they go at all. If it rained, I said, "God doesn't want me in Mass because He sent the rain." If I went to Mass, I looked for the shortest Mass where the priest spoke less. I would say what a tiring Mass, what a tiring priest, and I neither went to confession nor to Communion.

At the same time, I sat on the first row, with my low cut blouse and my miniskirt. There on the first row, I kept an eye on the priest. If the priest greeted the young people, I said this priest is a pedophile. If the priest walked with the same lady, I said this priest has a lover. "So shameless, look at the insolent, this immoral one", imagine with me, such a Catholic; who wants an enemy?

I said "look at those prudish ones boasting themselves as holy rollers, but they are worse than us" and I left the Mass after having spilled my poison.

The new age in my life

I went to have my tarot cards read, I was enslaved in "new age". I never read the Gospel, I never read the life of the saints, I said I hated the Bible, I hated St. Paul when he said: "women submit to your husbands"; I said "what does that wretch think, that they have not hit us hard enough to continue to be submissive."

I hated all of this and I left Mass on Sunday. To what? To the transcendental meditation courses, yoga, mental power, and to have astrologers read my astral chart. For a time brothers and sisters, I believed in reincarnation and spent a lot of money going where people "cleared" my mind and lay their hands on me in order to see my previous lives by doing regressions.

Can you imagine how dangerous it is to be laying hands on another person with a blank mind, and having hands laid on you? Do you know who entered my interior? None other than the devil. They laid their hands on me and told me to look into my previous lives and that they were going to heal my karma.

When I believed in reincarnation. I was a vegetarian; I did not eat meat, no animal. I was afraid I would eat a friend, father or aunt in a steak or roast, because they say that you can reincarnate in animals. When I was there I saw my great-grandmother, my parents, and all my relatives who came to meet me. When I was going towards that light, when I saw them, do you know what I said brothers and sisters? Oh they cheated me; they took all my money in all their deceits.

The devil made me his slave and his servant
When a person is not full of God, he ends up being full of the devil. That is what happened in my life to the point that I ended up being a defender of abortion, defender of euthanasia, and a destroyer of homes. I destroyed many of my friends' homes by telling them "don't be stupid, get another man, leave him." I ended up destroying many homes. The saddest thing was that I defended homosexual marriage; I said, "let them be happy, why not?"

I even defended euthanasia; do you know why I defended all of that brothers and sisters? *Because the devil made me his slave and his servant.* When one sins, the devil says, "well, now go and bring me your *mother, your brothers and sisters, your relatives, your friends, and everyone."*

For example, when I got caught up in witchcraft, where did I go? To the doors of hell, and I opened them and I went in. Who did I take with me? I invited my friends, my sisters, my nieces, my cousins, and my patients to go to witchcraft; I took all of them, I went there and I brought them all with me.

When I truly saw myself, oh how those things scream, what horror. My spiritual life was so sad, and regrettable; how I took care of my soul in such a way that in the end I no longer believed in anything.

I did not believe in the devil. I used to say that the devil was a lie, that he was an invention of the priests, that only the poor and uneducated believed in the devil. Ah, when I saw myself full of all those devils, oh what a shocking scare to see that sin is alive. A person that does not go to confession is simply frightful.

My father was also there

I continued to fall and while I was falling the people were not there anymore. I could hardly see them, they were buried between marshes. When they were between those marshes, I felt a great pain when I saw them scream. They screamed and cried; do you know why? They were very ashamed, because they had given the body, the Temple of the Holy Spirit to prostitution, to aberrations, to adultery, to all those things.

When I was looking at them, oh how they screamed. You cannot imagine the pain when I saw my father screaming, he was not like my mother, but just as I was. My father was the best to me, he was a modern father, cool, and we all drank. All seven children would go partying together every week with our father.

We all gathered those who liked beer and liquor, we danced, we went for rides and everything. He even gave us beer and liquor when we were very little, so that when we grew up, we wouldn't get drunk.

I used to say, "What a father I've got, he is a prize of a father." I felt very proud of my father. My father was a womanizer, he had many women, but none were permanent. My father would say that adultery was not a sin. He used to say, "What is sin?

It would be a sin if I left my wife or if I put my wife in second place, but my wife is a lady. If it were a sin, God would not have sent me here with so many hormones. No, sin is to fail to take advantage of the women. Poor women, how they become dishonorable, they no longer have dignity, they no longer know how much they are worth, they no longer have self-esteem, and they let themselves be fondled with such ease.

It is not but three flowers and four pretty words and they are already in the bed and let themselves be fondled; then they go from one hand to another, one tells his friend and then the friend takes his turn."

My father had a very sad concept of women and he used to say, "pity on the woman." Do you know what he said to my brothers and sisters? My boys, you have to be just as chauvinistic as your father, you must take advantage. But ask God for a good and holy woman for a wife, not a woman who goes around being fondled here and there. He would tell his three daughters, "do not become a dishonor; you must be worthy women, women of a single man with the sacrament on top. Did you hear me my daughters, watch out!"

The most painful part of sinning is that we rot everything that is around us

That was the home where I was raised, but do you know what brothers and sisters? It is painful when one is in the presence of God.

The first pain is the answer one gives to the love of God, to see Him on the Cross, because in God there is no time, everything is present. In that eternal present, He is there, in each Eucharist, bleeding and crying out to the Father for us, praying the Our Father for us and begging us to stop sinning and come back to Him. That is what hurts the most, seeing Him bleeding for us and begging us.

Do you know what the second pain is? To see that sin does not remain in me. Not to say "I condemned myself, so what? What do you care?" That's what I said when the rosary fanatics went after me, the prayer loonies that I hated so much. I would say, "Well if I am condemned it is my problem, not your problem," but do you know what is the saddest thing? That sin does not remain in us.

When I sin I become damaged fruit and if I am damaged fruit, what do I do? *I rot everything that is around me,* what does a man have closest to him when he is sinning? *His children, his wife, his friends, relatives... so everything starts rotting.*

The pain of my father, as there was no time there, in that present, my father screamed of pain each time my brothers and sisters arrived drunk, each time they spent the money from the blessing of my nephews and their wives on partying, and liquor.

When they arrived drunk to hit their women and children, when they went crazy, my father screamed of pain, do you know why? Because it was the same home that we had seen, my father would arrive drunk and start hitting us; my mother would hide us, so that my father could not hit us.

Now, my brothers and sisters are repeating the same as my father. But do you know what was my father's greatest pain? My father screamed of pain, it was his torment, there in that cell, in that marsh, whenever my brothers slept with another woman, besides their wives; my father screamed of pain and it was his greatest torment.

However, I could not stay with my father. I continued to fall and do you know what my father screamed? He said, "thank you Lord, thank you, for those thirty-eight years of prayer from that holy woman that you gave me for wife. Thanks to her I was saved."

My mother used to be the other side of the coin

Imagine, my mother was a very poor woman, but in love with Jesus. She said, "I am in love with Jesus, I love Him with all my passion, that is why I look at your father with compassion and I want him to be saved. When I was in front of the Blessed Sacrament, He snatched me and took me to hell to show that your father was in hell. While he was still alive, the demons had a hold of him in alcoholism, prostitution and in womanizing.

When I saw him in hell, I took the Rosary, I touched your father and several men I saw there that were in the same case as your father and I pray every day so that your father is saved, my daughter. That is why I spoil him and I love him so much because your father gives me much pity."

I would say, "*no mother*, it is because you are stupid. What are you doing tolerating my father like that? Why don't you find someone else, you are pretty." My mother would say to me, "Shhh." When she put up her finger in front of her lips, it meant shut up my daughter, do not let the devil speak through your mouth.

I would get so angry when she did that to me. She would say to me, "my daughter, do you think that I am going to soil this body, here where God dwells, where I feel a fire in my heart of the love of God. I am happy because happiness is not a man, nor money, nor education. Happiness is only found when one has a personal encounter with the love of God. I had it and since then I have remained with the love of God."

I would tell my mother, "you are very brave." She kept herself up and very pretty. All the women whose husbands were unfaithful lived screaming, crying, emaciated but she was very pretty. Then my mother would say, "am I perhaps the one sinning, my daughter? No, I am at peace. I am not sinning, why wouldn't I be screaming? No, no, no, no, the one who has to scream is him because he is sinning."

"I am praying so he is saved my daughter," and my father thanked God for the prayers of my mother. I continued to fall, can you imagine, falling and falling and falling; when I fell onto a flat part, a mouth opened, a living mouth, a living hatred, and it sucked me in.

I was standing up and it sucked me in. I felt as if they had put me inside a mouth and I went in head first.

Thanks be to God someone grabbed me by my feet pulled me out, but then my body entered that frightful hole. Immediately a pile hurled on me, as if they were larvae or leeches, horribly impure spirits hurled themselves on me and they burnt me. For the first time, the sins that I had within me burnt me and I was burning terribly. There were no candles but I was being burnt frightfully, and do you know what was the worst thing? **That I could feel that the love of God was absent.**

It was very easy for me to proclaim myself an atheist. I proclaimed myself an atheist with my friends, I considered myself an atheist and very intelligent. I thought that if I died everything ended. *Incredibly, despite all of this, I thought I was right.*

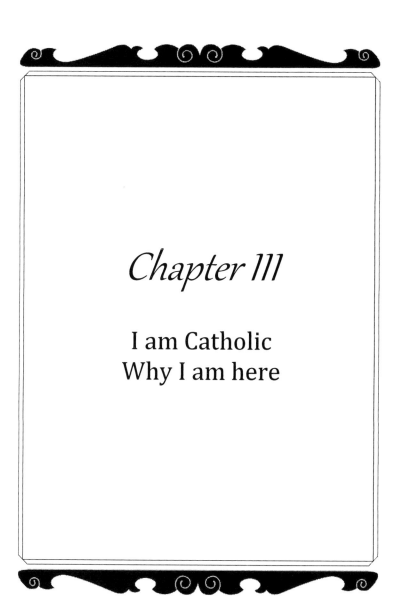

Chapter III

I am Catholic
Why I am here

I am Catholic, why I am here...

Then I had my judgment before God

It is very easy for an atheist to call themselves that while living in the love of God, but when they are there, where they do not feel the love of God, that is the worst torment.

When I was there, I began to scream; I was no longer an atheist, I saw souls in purgatory and I yelled, "please, get me out of here!" When I screamed to the souls, I began to hear how they screeched their teeth, screamed, groaned, and cried, thousands and thousands of people who were in that hole, in that marsh of hatred.

It gives me much pain when I realize that these are the people who had committed suicide. They were waiting for the time of life that they had not lived to go by to go through what I was going to go through there.

I saw them screaming and I saw so many young people, what a great pain.

I am not bad
I begin to scream, "please get me out of here, I have never stolen, killed, or hurt anyone. I gave food to the poor." I began screaming, "get me out of here, I am Catholic please get me out of here!"

When I screamed that I was Catholic, I saw a light. Can you imagine a light in the darkness? I saw a small staircase above the hole and on that staircase I saw my father and my mother. My father was on the first step, with very little light. Four steps above with a great light was my mother, beautiful, her clothes shining.

When I saw them I felt great joy and I began to scream, "dad, mom, please, get me out of here." When I screamed to them to get me out of there, my parents lowered their eyes and they saw me in that hole. What a great pain in their eyes, my father began to cry; he puts his hands on his head, and screamed, no, Lord, not my daughter, not my daughter." I was my father's favorite. My mother did not cry nothing took away the peace in her face, but she prayed and looked up; my father could not pray nor look up.

The responsibility of being parents
At that moment I realized that my parents were there because they were going to answer to our Lord for the home that they had given me. All parents are going to be at the judgment of their children, it does not matter if the son or the father dies first because there is no time over there, everything is present. Each

38

father and each mother are going to answer to our Lord for the home they have given their children and the mark they have left inside the children.

I was a great feminist and for the first time I was glad I was a woman. How hard is it for men to answer to our Lord because God demands them to be the authority? He demands them to love their children and gives holy authority, not violence to imprint their children, give them direction. The mark that a father leaves inside his children cannot be erased by anyone.

They begin asking my father, why weren't you a true Catholic? If you had been a true Christian your daughter would not be there. Why didn't you bless her every day? Look at all the blessings that you still owe your daughter. If you had given her these blessings, your daughter would not be there. Why didn't you teach your daughter to pray?

My father thought that my mother had to teach the children to pray. My father thought that being a good father was earning money in spite of poverty, bringing food home, sending us to school and giving us clothes; but that my mother should watch over the children.

They begin asking her, why didn't you give your daughter some of your time and listen to her about what she had done during the day? Why didn't you direct her misconducts. They begin to ask my father, why is your daughter a liar? Because you taught her how to lie when she was five years old. When they came to collect the money and you sent your daughter to say that you were not there, you gave her to the father of lies. They begin to tell my father, why is your daughter a feminist? Your drunkenness and ill treatments caused your daughter to be enraged against men.

Give thanks that your wife never planted hatred but taught your children to love you in spite of your drunkenness. But look the deception caused *by having a drunk father who came to mistreat her, caused her to become a feminist.* I begin to see how a man suffers.

They ask him, why didn't you develop your daughter's talents? And they looked at my mother with so much kindness. A woman's judgment, obviously when she is full of God not when she is in sin, goes to God. Do you know what a woman is? She is glass full of the tenderness of God.

When a mother with that tenderness, gives her breast to the baby, moves and the baby has trickling drops, do you know what happens? At that moment, the spirit of God is on the creature and in its mother.

The formation that a mother gives, a mother like that, whether the boy is very ugly or horrible; the mother says, "how beautiful my son, look how lovely my boy is, how tender, so intelligent, how he walks, see how he moves."

That causes the woman to be a shaper of humanity, that love and tenderness that God gives the creature through the mother makes the children be different and secure. Do you know what a woman is? A shaper of humanity. Do you know what the Devil did? He pulled women out of where we were so important because no one replaces a mother. He pulled women out to work, to support the homes. Who educates our children? The television, computer, and videogames. That is why we raise children with depression who want to commit suicide. That is what the Lord was showing me.

My judgment... and discovered who I truly was.

When I saw the pain of my parents, you can't imagine the pain that I felt. And I started to shout, "Please let me out of here, I am Catholic! I do not have to be here."

When I screamed that I was Catholic for the second time, I could hear a sweet voice, a very sweet voice. Everything was full of peace, the whole creation trembled with love, and these frightful creatures prostrate themselves in adoration. When I saw them prostrate, I was ashamed of myself, do you know why brothers and sisters? Because I was more arrogant than those demons that had prostrated themselves at the sound of the Lord's voice. Instead, do you know what I was saying?

I was swearing. These creatures lead you to be more arrogant and more sinful than them. I was swearing in the name of the Lord, I was saying to him, "why don't you listen to me God. I have asked for so much of you and received nothing in return." I was complaining and those creatures were trembling.

When those creatures went away because they could not resist the sweetness of the love; the voice said to me, "very well, the workmanship of each person will become evident.......it will be revealed with fire (1 Cor. 3,13-15). *If you are Catholic, tell me the commandments of God's law.*" Commandments, brothers and sisters, oh my God! I had no idea, you can't imagine my fright, I knew that there were Ten Commandments, but nothing more. I said, "now what do I do? What am I going to do?"

Ok, I know I am going talk my way out of the first commandment, that one I do know. I said, "The first one is to love God over all things, and to the neighbor as if the same." The voice said, "very well and have you loved him", and I shouted, "I have, I have." When they said to me "No!" All the saint's masks fall down to the floor, I stayed nude in all my hypocrisy and my falsity.

I was always a double person and hypocritical, my family did not even know that I was an atheist. For example: I was Catholic with the Catholics, atheist with the atheists, and with the separated brothers and sisters I was a free thinker. Oh my God! I had something for everyone. But now all my thoughts and feelings were revealed by the light. Look at an example, in the judgment there are no the thoughts or feelings. I used to tell my friends, "wow what a nice dress you look wonderful."

Inside I was thinking, she looks so disgusting. Or I would tell my friends, "You look so thin, are you on a diet?" Inside I was laughing and saying to myself, she looks like a pig. Over there, the thoughts speak first then the words, all the masks and the whole falsity fell down.

The voice told me, "no! **You have not loved your Lord** over all things, much less your neighbor as yourself. You made a God to suit your life, only remembering your Lord in moments of need and suffering. There you were running around, searching for your God. You were offering prayers, going to prayer groups and what did you accomplish, nothing.

Scarcely the blessing was fulfilled; you never fulfilled what you had promised."

Nothing was asked from you in return, everything was given to you in blessing, but you received it and never responded.

At a moment, they opened the book of my life

You never had word of honor, because you only had a god when you needed money. You were running after him to ask your God because your God was idolatry, your God the money. When they said to me that my God was money, I shouted; "but which money, on earth I left many debts," *and that was the last thing that I said*, because in that moment, they opened the book of life.

Can you imagine how wonderful God is? How much He loves us, how big our God's love is that we all are so special that he has a book for each of us. Our mothers have a photo of when we were one or two years old, but our Lord has a book. When he opened the book, I saw my entire life.

You cannot imagine how beautiful it is to see your whole life, from fertilization to the last moment of your life. This beautiful book began when the ovum and the sperm joined, and there is an explosion, a contact, and from this merger of cells from my parents I form like the most beautiful sun and illuminate the belly of my mother. What was this little sun, my soul, and from the same moment of fertilization, it did not even have brain; even scarcely now these cells begin splitting. But I was already speaking with God. All creatures from the moment of fertilization, speak with God; and the Lord showed me the "humanity" of the embryo.

There it is, the lack of humanity hurts the Lord. The Lord gives talents to every person, so that we can be employed at God's kingdom, at God's Project.

I began to grow and so did the sin in my life
When I was a child, until I begun to sin, I wanted to help people. I felt sorry for the poor, I was crying for the suffering of others and I wanted the world to be good. My mom had helped me well in these virtues and had taught me as it is necessary to teach children, to be caring. My mother was taking me to visit patients, to help people, and I loved people.

When I began to sin, what a huge pain it was, my brothers and sisters; this beautiful soul that loved God and people began to sin. This white, beautiful soul, full of the living water of God's love, began to fill with sin, the living sin. I became a fibber, lazy, bad disciple, and so I was filling myself with bad things. My soul was as a Dalmatian, one sin was opening the door to another, a small lie to a bigger lie, and so on.

I was filling with sin, and my soul was getting dirty; as I was sinning, I was losing my love for God.

I was sinning like if you throw a glass of mud into a glass with water, what happens to the water? The water becomes cloudy. What is this cloudy love? It initially has an interest in loving God but then that well-being is given, including money, and everything is

44

going well you begin to forget about God. I was not loving God for being God, I was loving myself and did not initiate to answer to God with love.

When I saw the book of my life, I knew that it was time to accept the reality of my sin.

That's how our God demonstrated it to me, commandment by commandment, how cruel I was, a rebel, and how I didn't take care of my faith.

"If we claim to be without sin, we deceive ourselves and the truth is not in us "
1 Jn 1,8

How I was a bad wife with my husband, when I got married. God showed me when my husband was single because he had lots of money, he was my Love, my life, my sweet heart. I always dressed up and took care of myself for him. As soon as we got married, he was no longer my sweet heart but a degenerate, a bastard and blatant, worthless and good for anything.

God showed me that I was no longer affectionate with him or caring. My mom always told me, "daughter to win your husband's heart, you should always be affectionate and caring." I would always say, "oh yeah, he should be taking care of me because I always work."

My mom told me, "tell him to help you when he gets home." I would tell my mom I don't think so, he always gets home late and sleepy. God showed me that I was unfaithful to my husband because of who my husband was when I was single. He was an alcoholic and mean and I still accepted him the way he was.

He met a sweet girl that would listen to him, who was lovely, caring and who spoiled him. But as soon as I got married, God showed me that when my husband got home, he would find me with electronic devices around my stomach to lose weight, with massage devices, looking like trash and in a bad mood, fighting with him, yelling at him and I never again listened to him.

God showed me that I participated in my husband leaving the house, he wasn't even home yet and I would already be asking him for money.

I help Satan throw others into hell using my words

God showed me my children, imagine what a mother who is an atheist can give her children, I gave them death. My children only cared about what was in style, the latest toys and devices. I went with my husband to get money loans because I didn't want my children to be poor like I was. I wanted my children to have all the latest toys and stylish clothes that I didn't have when I was a child because I was very poor.

God showed me that my children had a bcrib made of gold but they didn't have a father or a mother that gave them love and guidance. When my children were afraid, they could do nothing but hold it in and have insecurities. My daughter doesn't know what a hug from a mother feels like and she didn't know how to hug. My daughter always had that necessity for a mother's hug, she finally realized she had to find a mom who she could go to because she didn't have a mom, can you imagine how embarrassing that was?

My daughter had everything except a mother, but God in his mercy healed her. God has healed her emotional injuries and has restored her, but the pain that one feels in hurting their children cannot be restored by anyone. God showed me how much harm I caused humanity with the mere capacity that I had to give advice to people, I destroyed families. God showed me how many souls

I helped Satan throw into hell using my words, **how much bad advice I gave, and how many times I laughed at people**. What authority did I have to laugh at people and to humiliate people?

He showed me all the people that where in my life that I had hurt and what has happened in their lives. I am going to talk about two of them. One of them, a young patient of mine from when I would volunteer to help people in need. He was very poor. Yes, it's good that I volunteered and worked for free to help people in need but when one does not have God in their hearts even the good things can cause harm.

I would tell him "Yahir, Yahir you need to enjoy life, have lots of women in your life, but don't be stupid...use a condom. Don't go have sex without a condom, if you don't have the money to purchase them I will give you money, so that you always use a condom."

God showed me, that this patient of mine, who I treated growing up until he was thirteen, started having a sexual life at twelve. At age fifteen in Medellin, Colombia; God showed me that with condom and all, he was infected with AIDS. He did not know he was infected with AIDS until he was an adult.

He went to live with a young girl and they had a child together. The child died at two and half years old. Why did he die? Because he had pneumonia as a result of AIDS. God demonstrated how powerful every word can be and the damage they cause.

With every person you have been involved with, *God* ***will show you the footprints that you have left in every person***.

Chapter IV

Yes, I use to be Catholic...

Yes, I used to be Catholic...

But my life was filthy with sin

I had my judgment. Commandment by commandment to brothers and sisters. I didn't even pass one, he showed me how I was a bad daughter, and how I was mean and ungrateful.

I used to think that I was a powerful woman but I was lost in sin.

The enemy, having seen that he has a little time left, is leading humanity to the worst things, to being beasts, slaves of instincts, of pleasure, who only think about pleasure, and being in the state of pleasure.

He takes humanity to the most terrible of places, to do the beastliest of things. Do you know what hurt me the most? To see the most perverse generation of all times, do you know which this is? This one, where the women are so "intelligent".

We have reached so many positions and we feel better than men. In all the wars that man has fought from the beginning until now, humanity has never seen so much blood spilled like the women have spilled in the last 50 or 60 years; with daily abortions, the babies' deaths have been increasing. Earlier generations of women, as my mother, remained filled with God, faithful in their hearts and fought up to the last moment for their children and husbands, until they were saved.

Nowadays, it is more difficult for women, the demon extracts us to work and our children remain alone without anyone to educate them. At work, women turn into prostitutes, they have lovers after they leave their husbands, to have others, and to have abortions. What a pain for our God, that the intelligent women are spilling so much blood, and the worst thing of all, do you know what a satanic sacrifice is? It is a satanic sacrifice to sacrifice a son, this is what hurts God the most.

There are times when women are worse than men, unfortunately. I was a feminist, liberated from having a man.

What spiritual treasures do you bring?
Do you know the first thing God asked me? Did I bring any spiritual treasures? They knew how empty my hands were, I was not taking anything, and they were saying to me what good is it to say that you had your apartment or your office. What did it serve you? That you were considered to be a professional with a

lot of success. So much cult to your body, so much money spent in your body. What did it get you?

Could you bring the dust of a brick? Could you bring your body that you idolized so much? Everything that you had was given in blessing; **much was given to you, so much will be required of you.**

I was realizing how much I was wasting my life and our Lord was showing me all the hungry people that were dying in the entire world. He showed me all the money that I spent at the gym, in jewels, in expensive restaurants, in squandering, in binges, and in clothes that I was buying and was not using. You of stone, insensitive before the pain of your brothers and sisters.

After being married in a catholic church committing adultery, God was showing me how painful it was for a child to have 3 fathers and for a mother to have two children from the first marriage, two children from the second marriage and to have to raise a child from a third marriage, the pain and chaos that we have caused.

> You know what I say brothers and sisters, a sin against marriage is terrible. *It's better not to have eyes and a tongue, before you advise somebody to destroy a marriage.*

It is a mortal sin to come between a marriage. That's when God asks me, "what have you done with the talents that I have given you." Can you imagine the talents? I had forgotten I had a soul much less talents.

I was Catholic in my own way. I believed in God, but I had my own gods.

When they start to ask me in the first commandment to love God over all things, they showed me the love of loves, who loves us so much. I would approach God not to love Him but to ask for money because my God was money. They start showing me the person who eats his body and drinks his blood unworthy, who eats and drinks his own sentence. I would go and receive the Eucharist without confessing, with moral sin, thinking I was a saint because I thought I didn't commit sins.

I would receive the Eucharist with my lucky charm on my wrist, grasping the devil, with a rabbit's foot in my purse, and birth control inserted in my body so that I wouldn't get pregnant. ***The worst thing was that I thought that I was good and everything was fine the way it was.***

God would show me what an evil woman I was to choose how many children I wanted to raise and how many I wanted to murder. He would show me that I would receive the Eucharist in excommunication, because a woman who aborts and receives the Eucharist is under excommunication.

Why? Because all Catholics are in God's heart but a person who defends abortion, who votes for a politician that is for abortion or a person who aborts removes themselves from God's heart and is in excommunication, in other words they will not enter into heaven because heaven is in God's heart.

I would go and receive the Eucharist with birth control in my body when I had heavy hemorrhages and blood clots. Women know our menstrual period very well. God would show me when I had those heavy hemorrhages and had birth control in my body, the blood clots would not stop. Those were the microscopic babies that were reproduced but couldn't be implanted. They were released from my body and God shows that there's nothing more secure and safe than a mother's womb for a baby's safety.

A mother is willing to die for their child and I was a baby killing machine and I would approach and receive the Eucharist like this.

I couldn't deny myself the truth. I was a bad Catholic….Even when I thought the contrary

God showed me my sin of idolatry. What idolatry? The money, what idolatry? My body, what idolatry? My friends, how I loved to party with my friends and drink liquor because I was "brave". My husband would go out and drink with his friends and I would go out with my friends.

God showed me *the pain of the consequences of my sins with the world*. How many souls I had destroyed when I used to talk about the priest. God said, "with what authority do you talk about my anointed priests and judge them, exalting yourself as God.

That was something I didn't know. **I finally saw my sad truth**, my life was a filthy mess.

Chapter V

It was true, I had never killed...

It was true, I had never killed...

But I supported Satan with the blood of abortion

Committed from the age of thirteen to the last moment of my life. Why from the age of thirteen? Because the most astute thing that the devil did with me was to remove me from sacramental confession. I used to say, "I do not confess to a priest, to a sinner, a homosexual man, a man worse than I. Forget it, I confess alone." All the sins from the age of thirteen, when I had my last confession, onwards, came out to get me.

When I was thirteen, I was a town girl in my country, we lived really far from the capital in a town about seven hours away. In my town, we were very poor, but we were all poor and we lent each other things. If a neighbor did not have beans one would lend him the beans.

One would borrow things, we were all poor, but we lived beautifully. All were believers who went to Mass, all had love and compassion. But when they brought me to the capital, I learned. I was put in a school for rich girls, for the first time I knew power, money, how beautiful people looked all dressed up, the fine clothes, the pretty shoes and I began to envy all that and wish I had a lot of money to have the same things they did.

We began to drink, I would listen to their conversations, and see how cool they were. They were promiscuous ("handed them over to their passions..." Rom. 1; 28-32) because they slept with their boyfriend or friends. They went dancing and for rides; I began to see all that as cool. Regrettably with them I partook in witchcraft and card readings.

One sin opened the door to another sin, when I began to sin. At this point, I could no longer stand my mother. She seemed ridiculous and old-fashioned. I used to say that my mother was Fred Flintstone's mother. I would say, "What bad luck, I have a mother who is poor, uneducated, and old-fashioned. Why didn't God give me a mother like these girls who have so much money, live happily and let them go anywhere at thirteen.

My friends started having abortions and I began to see abortion as normal. My friends made me feel like a coward and like I couldn't do anything because I did not want to sleep with anyone. I was a virgin and they made me feel like the black sheep of the group because I did not sleep with their friends. Do you know why I did not sleep with their friends? Because my mother was holy and prayed for me which made me be afraid of not doing the same as they did.

But I did like what they did and I followed them and backed them up in many things, but not in that.

I was thirteen and was already familiar with many sins; I ditched school, went to see R-rated movies, I was rude to my mother, I was a bad student, I copied, I cheated, I was greedy, and I was envious. The worst of all was to have fallen into witchcraft, because of what I got into **I could not pray again. I began to be annoyed at Mass**, bored and tedious; I became depressed, and daydreamed about fears, and desired to commit suicide.

You cannot imagine how dangerous it is to go to those things, when one believes in witchcraft and omens; the devil comes into one's head and begins to damage one's unconscious and subconscious mind until one has depressions and anguishes. Well, I was thirteen and I was dead. From then on, I began to sin all my life, in many things, and the saddest thing is that the more I sinned, the more holy I felt because my conscience was numbed to the point that nothing was a sin.

When somebody told me that what I did was a sin, they became my enemies. What sin? Old Holy Roller, prudish, rosary fanatic, go pray over there, under the priest's skirt, and let us live our lives as we wish. I hated prayerful people. Why did I hate my mother? Because my mother prayed, spoke to me about God; and good behavior.

As I got older, I suggested that other women not be fools and to have an abortion in order to live out their lives.

The Beast tells us that the bad is good and we believe it.

God showed me that I was doing what Satan wanted me to say and do. I was a dreadful person when I talked bad about the priests. God said, "you are the one that aborts and talks bad about my priests I will show you an abortion."

Every woman that has had an abortion, God will show us what we don't see, when a woman is in labor and under anesthesia. He will demonstrate what great pain God feels for the doctor, who he loves for taking care of his brothers and sisters and the sacrifice of caring for other's health.

God showed how the doctor cuts the baby's legs and how the baby yells. How the doctor cuts their little arms and destroys the baby's head. Then just throws the baby in a can, unconcerned and calm like nothing happened. A chef feels worse when killing a chicken and cooking it, than a doctor feels when killing an innocent baby, destroying it into pieces and throwing it away.

God shows the baby's cry, even though the innocent baby only had a second of life. He/she already could talk to God and the baby's cry is so loud that all of God's creation could hear the cry. God cries, hurting with pain every time an abortion takes place. If millions of abortions are taking place each day, imagine how hurt God gets.

I thought I wasn't an adulterer...But I was wrong again.

I said: "Here I will not fail, because I never had an affair." I was wrong, they showed me that when I walked around showing off my cleavage that I wanted men to see and desire me.

I made them sin and I was promoting adultery. I would tell my friends: "Don't be dumb. If your husbands cheat on you, you can do the same. I was truly a hidden adulterer, but *I couldn't deny it anymore.*

God shows how the devil approaches us through the media. If you want to be happy, sleep around. In God's eyes, that's not making love. Making love is in the Sacrament of marriage. God has nothing against pleasure when it's within the marriage.

The Sacrament of marriage is important, when a couple is getting married two walk in but three walk out because when the couple receives the Eucharist in the Sacrament of marriage, God joins the couple in their hearts, and only death can separate a marriage.

When one of us decides to get married, we don't ask the Holy Spirit who we should marry but instead we go out like crazy then get married. No one can separate a marriage. A sin against marriage is a sin against the trinity because the Father, the Son and the Holy Spirit are witnesses to that union.

When a couple gets married, a fire is lit on the bed, the fire of the Holy Spirit, and on the dining table. What's the first thing God asks a parent? What did you give your child? Did you give them God? If the person was married, they should say yes. "Yes, Lord I gave them to you because my child was fertile in your Holy Spirit on your Holy bed because the fire lit on the bed is now a Holy bed."

Satan uses the media to impact the youth especially, and shows them that it's alright for teenagers to start having sex.

I did not have an abortion, but I recommended it, as an option to other women.

God would look at me, with great pain as I supported the idea of teenagers having sex. I would tell teenagers not to be stupid, that getting married was the worst mistake they could make, and that they should enjoy life. But one thing for sure, use condoms so you don't get pregnant.

You know what's sad? When a teenage girl ends up pregnant. No one has ever done a study on how many teenage girls have gotten pregnant using condoms. However I had a lot of experience with a lot of people that I helped pay for abortions because I gave them the advice to have an abortion. *I considered myself to be a good person because I would help them pay for their abortion*.

I would pay for my family members and close friends to have abortions. They all got pregnant using a condom. A teenager who has an abortion is never the same. God showed me that for every child that is murdered, a demon is unleashed; an evil demon sealed in hell with God's blood when he descended to hell.

That's why a lot of people are confused with the New Era, thinking that all religions are the same and Catholics who are over there lighting candles and putting themselves in yoga positions are making a brutal mistake. People say that Satan does not exist, what a terrible mistake that is.

Nobody can imagine to what point humanity allowed abortion. When a young girl gets pregnant, it's as if a big leech is wrapped around her. She doesn't see a solution, it's like she is under anesthesia and her only solution is to sacrifice the baby. As soon as the young girl kills the baby she wakes up but the beast has already taken the baby. You should see the horrible beasts that are feeding and enjoying the abortions; I supported all of those.

> I forgot an important detail; I had a soul and it needed nourishment.

How many times have we spoken too much and allowed our tongue to become an instrument of destruction? Adultery wasn't only physical, but also emotional.

I couldn't hide anything. The finite moment had come and I had to accept who I really was.

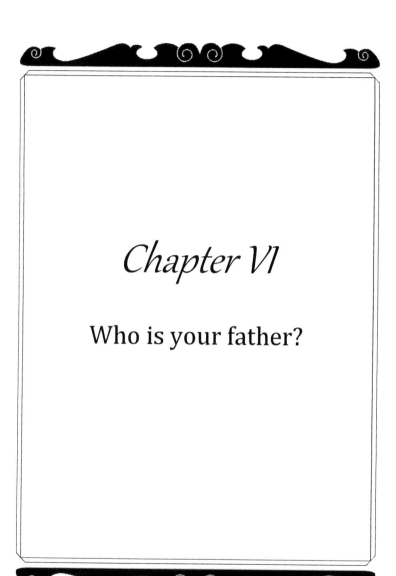

Chapter VI

Who is your father?

68

Who is your father...

God or Satan

God showed me that lies are not white or black, lies are lies and Satan is the father of lies.
The truth was that the way I was living was not in obedience to God, but to Satan.

I walked with the father of lies, Satan was my father.

Can you imagine my reaction when God showed me that because of my love for money, I didn't get separated. Why? I could only think that because of my love for money, I did not get separated from my husband, because my lawyer would ask me for 40% of my money. 40%, what a bastard! He didn't have to sleep with my drunk husband like I had to all those nights. I'd rather keep the money.

God showed me that I loved money so much that I let myself have a price. My husband and I were in ruins because my husband touched dirty money. What is dirty money? Dirty money is received at the cost of narcotics, kidnapping, and prostitution.

This money cursed my husband; he had to flee from our house because they were chasing him. He sold his house very cheap and started a different business in Bogota. They offered him some easy money; can you imagine where, in Bogota, this money came from.

Now I had money, but my life was empty

It was drug money. I told my husband not to accept that money because it was wrongfully earned but he told me, "if I do this business, I will take you on a vacation Gloria." I said, "really?" In an instant, I lost my morality.

God showed me that because we touched that money, I was an accomplice of all the children, homes and families that were destroyed because of the drugs; each and every person that was addicted to those drugs.

You can't imagine how terrible it is to touch dirty money. I had money, but no life.

**Horrible!
I lived in true chaos and it was time to accept it.**

There was no place where I could hide my lies and sins, not even in the deepest part of my conscience.

I kept on sinning, speaking badly about people, not loving people, being envious, covetous, and I wanted money to be happy, I was filling up with sin; when I was sinning, I was not thinking of others, or God. My father was Satan and I was barely finding out.

70

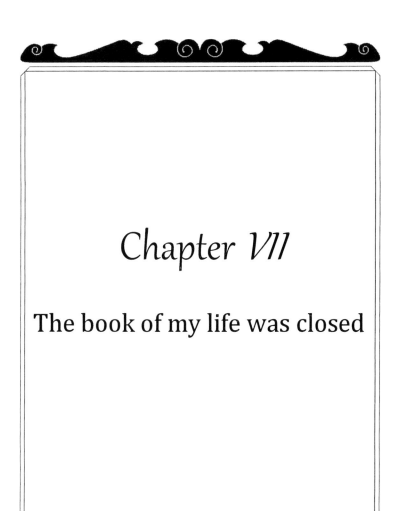

Chapter *VII*

The book of my life was closed

Then I began to scream...

Try to imagine when the book of life was closed on me. I started to ask all the saints to save me but when I stopped naming all the saints, I saw that there was nothing else that could be done for me. I raised my eyes to meet the eyes of my mother. When I saw my mother, I said, "Mom! Mommy, how embarrassing that I have condemned myself."

I felt a horrible and painful emptiness. No one could help or intercede for me.

The book was closed and there was nothing I could do.

A horrible shame, pain, and a cold loneliness went through my being. I had used my life to destroy my husband, my children, and my friends...Oh how many people did I destroy!

I thought to myself, "Where I am going, my mother will never see me again." But then my Mother was granted to do something special, she raised both of her fingers and pointed up and signaled me to look up. I don't know what I saw but the veil over my eyes was swept out, my spiritual blindness was gone.

I saw a special, beautiful moment in my life. When a patient of mine told me, "look Doctor, you are materialistic women but one day you are going to need Him in your life. When you are in immense danger whatever it may be, ask Jesus Christ to cover you with His blood and He will never abandon you because he paid that price with His blood for you." With immense pain, *I shouted, Jesus Christ have mercy on me"*, and something very special happened.

Chapter *VIII*

Lord, have mercy on me!

Lord, give a second chance...

F ather forgive me, give me a second chance. That was the most beautiful moment because He fell into that light, took me out of that hole and put me on a plain surface. He told me with lots of love, "you're going to return.

You're going to have your second chance but not because of your family's prayers, because it's normal that they cry and pray for you, but because of all the people that are not related to you who are crying and praying for you."

You know what I saw, my brothers and sisters, the power of prayers and intercession. *For the first time, I understood that it was communion of the saints.* In my country, even though there is lots of suffering, when the news came out that I was struck by lightning a lot of people prayed for me.

Our Lord is pleased when people stop praying for their husband, children, or house and start praying for people they don't even know. A lot of people prayed for me and their souls were lit with the fire of the Holy Spirit; they started to rise like flames in the darkness.

I saw how the Virgin Mary gathers, in her left hand, all the prayers of the Columbian people and with her right hand gathered all the prayers of the Saints. The Saints are praying all the time and intercede for us.

In that instant the Virgin Mary kneeled down and intervened for me. I was to return because in that moment I proclaim Jesus Christ as my savior. I had never known Jesus Christ as my savior. That's when I yelled, "God have mercy for me."

Cried and prayed for me: Save my spiritual sister!

But why am I here my brothers and sisters? Because the poorest of poor was a huge flame, in my country there is a Saint, my brothers and sisters, a farmer in the North end of my country. In the snowy hills of Santa Martha, very poor he didn't even have bread on his table, the guerrilla ate his chickens and the harvest burned. He didn't have money to pay the guerrilla so the guerrilla asked for his oldest child.

However, this farmer got ready on Sunday, very nice, with his two kids and they walked really far for hours and hours. It had drizzled they showed up all wet at the farmhouse. I despised farmers because they didn't have an education or money. In that farmhouse, they were celebrating the Eucharist when the farmer entered very humbly. He put his face on the sand, his forehead on the ground and told our Lord:

"*Lord! Lord! Thank you for life, thank you for my health, thank you for my children. Lord, I thank you that Colombia will become a good country. That Colombia will love you and that the world will love you, Lord*".

When the farmer got out of church, after he received the Eucharist, he bought bread and salt. He wrapped the bread in a half newspaper article called, The viewer (El Espectador); there was a picture of me burnt in the center, the farmer grabbed the bread, looked at my face and *started crying*.

He didn't know how to read very well, yet he read the news about my accident and he cried like I was his daughter.

He fell to the floor and asked our Lord:

"*Lord, Lord have mercy on my little sister. Lord, Lord save her. Lord if you save my sister, I promise you! I'll go to the sanctuary of Boja and fulfill a promise but please save my sister Lord*".

Can you imagine this farmer who didn't have any money to eat but offered to cross a country for me? When he prayed, he *called me sister*. Another person might have said at least that happened to a woman like that and not to the poor, but not this farmer, he shook the Lord's heart.

The Lord pointed to him and he told me, "that's what love for others means. You are going to go back."

You will have your second chance
In that moment, the Lord gave me a mission.

He told me, "you are not going to repeat it a thousand times but a **thousand times a thousand**. There are those that will hear you and don't want to change, but they are going to be judged with even more severity like you are going to be, next time.

There is not a worse deafness than the one that doesn't want to hear and not a worse blindness than the one that doesn't want to see. My brothers and sisters, I finish with this. This is not a threat, this is a Lord in love and he doesn't get tired of begging. Do you know why I am here my brothers and sisters? Because the Lord loves each and every one of you. The Lord is trying to give each of you a second opportunity, not just me.

God is lending you this mirror
If you die, in this moment, where will you go? Do you see how much he loves you? The only thing that is definite, in this life, is death. Look brothers and sisters, His love is so powerful that he has me here. Maybe I am here, in this moment for the love of my Lord and for the love of you all.

Brothers and sisters, don't forget, if I am here today it's because the Lord loves you and wants all of you in heaven. We want to go to heaven even after hurting others: being unfaithful, partying, drinking, prostituting, and then we say let's go to heaven. No, my brothers and sisters, the Lord wants us as Saints, that's why He is here begging all of you.

My experience isn't unique; it has happened to many others. What God is doing is lending you a "mirror" to view others and my judgment. God wants to see you next to Him!

You can make one of the most important decisions in your life right now by telling Him that you want to be saved.

You decide!

I have a dream, my dream is that when we die, we will all meet in heaven, hug each other and say, "hi, my brothers and sisters. Remember when we saw each other over there." How beautiful it will be to see each of you in heaven. You have my prayers as long as I am alive and even after I die, God Bless everybody.

INVITATION

Dear brothers or sisters,

If while reading this testimony you felt God inside you and felt a new urge to forgive, to repent from sinning and to change the way you live, then it is time to make a decision.

Today is the day in which you give yourself up to Christ, so that he can save you, forgive your sins and govern your life.

I want to ask you for a favor because we want the Lord to talk to us more in this moment of prayer. Please close your eyes for a few seconds, that these seconds become the seconds of faith. We are silent so that the Lord can talk to our hearts. Close your eyes for a few seconds so you can see with the eyes of faith.

I want to ask you a question, with your eyes closed. Our sister shared what the Lord told her, what she saw and heard in her judgment; if death or judgment came for you today are you ready? What explanation are you going to give the Lord, think about it, think in your heart and let the Lord talk to you.

What explanation are you going to give to the Lord for your wife, husband, mother, children, or brother? How are you going to respond? Think about it with your eyes closed.

Our sister said that she called to the Lord, "save me, my Lord. I have sinned, have mercy of me." With your eyes closed I would like to ask you: have you ever told God, "Lord, save me" Have you ever told Jesus, "I want you to be my savior, Lord" have you ever told God, "**God, enough sinning**, it's enough Lord, it's enough Lord!"

I want to give you a personal invitation, if you want to take advantage of this moment that the Lord has talked to you. If it has been years since you have been to confession, if you have never asked the Lord to save you, to transform you, to forgive all of your sins.

If you are one of these people, with your eyes closed and say, "I want to ask you for forgiveness in this moment." If you are a woman, a man or a teenager that has lived in sin and wants to ask the Lord for forgiveness, that today the Lord will save your life, kneel down in this moment my brothers and sisters and sisters.

Take advantage of the opportunity that our sister has brought us; the second chance that the Lord gave her, He is giving it to you today.

We don't want to wait for our daughter, son husband, wife, father or mother to die in order to love them; proclaim Jesus.

If you have decided to do this, say this prayer from the deepest part of your soul and let the Lord Himself inhabit your heart.

Prayer of Commitment
"Dear Lord, forgive me. While reading this testimony, I cried various times because it was like I

was reading about my life. My soul is filled with misery and sin. Dear Lord! Have mercy on me and give me an opportunity.

I have failed you so much and the worst part is that I thought that everything was ok. I have used masks of hypocrisy and have lied to people about my life. Lord how false I have been, forgive me and make me a new child.

I have been a terrible Catholic, conforming to only go to church while thinking it was permissible to do whatever I wanted with my life.

Dear Lord, I saw my life reflected in Gloria in many ways, like a mirror. Forgive me, I beg you. I have been a horrible person who hasn't known how to love you in a true way. Lord, change me and have pity on me.
Amen."

Now start to calm down. If you wish to keep praying then do so! First keep praying then you can continue reading this book.

Now, let's keep moving.

Invitation
"If this testimony has been a blessing from God, He is touching your heart; get close to Jesus Christ.

Do it through confession with a priest, read the word of God, look to serve in your parish, pray the rosary, integrate yourself in a group or ministry at your church. More than that, look to grow the ministry in regard to the Holy Mass so that every day when you receive the Eucharist, you receive the Lord and Savior. Renew your covenant between you and Him.

Have faith that God will transform your life and that you will enjoy that life in abundance, because he came to give us his grace through his death and resurrection.

In this moment, I recommend some additional material that can help you:
1- If you want to learn about our faith, I recommend the book "Catholic Defend Your Faith."

2- If you are starting to walk in the faith, I recommend "I am Catholic, So What!"

Obtain it at www.anewevangelization.com

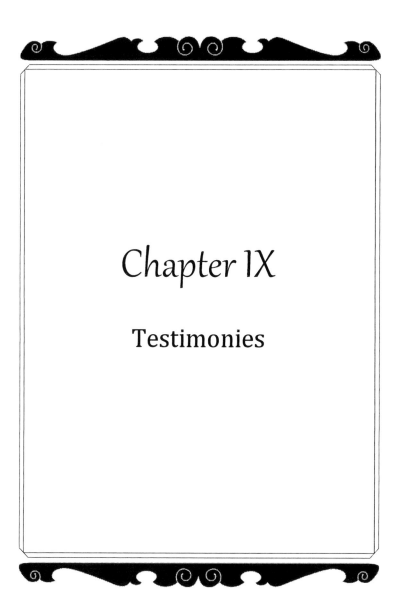

Chapter IX

Testimonies

T hank you brothers and sisters for continuing to read this book. Now I will share with you some of the hundreds if not thousands of testimonies from fellow Christians that have read the message of Gloria Polo. It is wonderful to see how many lives Jesus is able to transform through the Holy Spirit.

These testimonies will strengthen you in your faith even more.

I. Oh God! I am still in shock from this testimony

Yesterday I received the Testimony of Dr. Gloria Polo. Thanks to God, I think it is the first testimony from an average person that really speaks to me. We know other preachers, books, etc. That evangelize, catechize, and teaches us, But the experiences of Dr. Gloria Polo are without a doubt a true demonstration of the Mercy of God.

In conclusion, I thank God for his patience, and for believing in us even when sometimes we don't believe in Him. Watch out now that you have received this warning, the Holy Spirit may aid us in changing the lives of those who need help. Oh God! I am still in shock from this testimony. Sorry Lord, blessed are you. Help us to meditate and reflect on your love.

"Eternal Father, I offer the body and blood, the soul and divinity of your Beloved Son, our Lord Jesus Christ, for our sins and those of the rest of the world. By his passion, have mercy on us." Holy Mary, pray for us.

Emi

II. What will our children inherit?

I believe that Dr. Gloria Polo is very courageous for giving us her testimony. She invites us to reflect upon what we have done and are doing. It doesn't matter to her what people think of her.

It is important to grasp the essence of what she is saying. God is there! We should have Him close to us, constantly in our lives every minute of every day; not to ask Him for things, but to thank Him first.

Alice

III. Thank you, now I don't think about suicide.

Now I want to live in order to change. Dr. Gloria, I want to express my infinite gratitude for your testimony which has changed my life.

I was a lost soul that wanted to find its way again, to have the wonderful communication that I had with God when I was only a child but lost it by being weak. I was close to ending my life, but because of God's love for me I did not. In an inexplicable way I began to read about the apparitions of the Virgin Mary, then about the souls of purgatory and then I found your testimony, which helped me to no longer think about suicide.

Thank you for your testimony, inspired by God. You have given my soul the strength and will power to not only live on, but to right the wrongs that I have committed. God bless you and pray for me that my soul will be thankful.

Now I know what the Eucharist and prayer are really about... I believe this is the second chance that God has given me.

Patricia

IV. God has changed my life and taken me out of the swamp

Good day and may God bless you all. Yesterday I saw the testimony of Gloria Polo and I congratulate her for what she does. Some of us have testimonies of how God has changed our lives, but don't tell others. God is so merciful with us his children. God changed my life, when I was drowning in the swamp God changed me, I was spiritually dead. He helped my marriage and everything changed for the better thanks to God.

May God Bless you all

V. I finally see my errors

I was impacted by the experience of Dr. Gloria Polo. I also received a second chance through the presence of my daughter; she was born with many difficulties and it was only after this that I saw all my errors. Even to this day I continue to ask for forgiveness. Thank God for His divine mercy.

Luisa

VI. I cannot contain my tears

Dr. Gloria I am welling up inside. I am at work and cannot contain my tears. I had to stop what I was doing without finishing. I thank God for the person who sent me this testimony and allowed me to consciously see the reality of the life I was leading.

I give thanks to God for this experience which vibrates throughout the world for the glory of God.

I ask that God make me an instrument of his peace by seeing your testimony and showing it to others. How deeply it reached me, I hope it does the same for others so that they can see what God has intended for us; a path in this world, a mission that everybody has to go through.

Thank you Dr. Gloria for your testimony and for your courage. I ask God to help you reach many others that need your testimony "Standing Before God: The Judgment." It is something I will recommend to many others.

Martha

VII. Thank you for denouncing the reality of sin in which we live

I am very impressed by your testimony. When I heard it I began to see the reality that God loves us and gives us an opportunity every day to get closer to him, but we live in the land of sin and blind ourselves from seeing how far away from God's grace we live.

I have been speaking to my friends about this important book, especially in this society where abortions occur along with many different sins which keep us away from salvation.

I congratulate Dr. Gloria Polo for her particular way of expressing her wonderful experience because not only did it change her life, but those with whom she shares her story.

Alexandra

VIII. I believed I was a good person...

I saw the testimony of Dr. Polo this afternoon and I am in awe! I want to show this to all of my family, because it makes you want to reflect upon your life based on the way she says it.

Sometimes we believe we're good enough; because we do not kill or steal, but we are not helping others get closer to God. He will judge us on this as well! It is great hearing of Gloria Polo and I wish to know how to get the book and DVD "Standing Before God: The Judgment."

Christin

IX. I felt the desperation of being there

Dear Gloria,
I am speechless after hearing your testimony. I felt the Holy Spirit dwelling in me, I felt what you said: fear, terror, and desperation upon the possibility of losing myself and not being able to escape the darkness.

I believe that the whole world should know of your testimony. I ask myself: How much can God forgive? I always ask God to give us an opportunity, I ask God for His mercy and that He allows us to recognize our wrongs in order to spend eternity with Him.

May God bless you and allow others to listen to you, to learn and read as well. That we may see that we need to fix ourselves before we fix others. I ask God for His company and that of the Holy Virgin Mary in her intercession.

Mary Ann

X. Spiritual Fruits

After seeing part of your testimony, a couple married by law for 12 years with two girls decided to get married the Church. This happened on the 25th of November in the Church of "Our Lady of Candles" in Uruguay. May God bless Gloria and those who know her message.

Mariana

XI. Promote this testimony

I have just seen the testimony of Dr. Polo, I have a background in Catechesis and I am sure that what she says comes straight from God.

I am in the process of converting myself after a mission to a small place in my country. I was found by the embrace of Jesus Christ through the intercession of prayer.

I have found that the words of Gloria strengthen me in my prayer and adoration of the Eucharist and the fundamental factors of my relationship with Our Lord Jesus Christ.

We have the responsibility of spreading this testimony to others so that it may reach their hearts.

In God we trust.

James

XII. Stay strong

When I was 14-15, I heard the testimony of Gloria in a prayer group from a friend of my mom and I was very shocked. I lost myself over time, but now at 23 I have come back after hearing it again. To those of you who have lost their way and are trying to fix it in order to stay on the path; it gets difficult but it is worth it in the end.

Lourdes

XIII. Let us go towards Jesus' feet, there is still time

Thank God for Gloria Polo and allowing her to be the mirror of a great woman. I saw her when I was young and it is great to live with God and have Mary as my shield.

Let us not wait anymore! Teenagers let us go to Jesus' feet, for there is still time! He is the way out of this world, filled with abortion and promiscuity. Only God is King like the Word of God says.

Saul

XIV. Thank you and lets move forward

I am speechless. It was wonderful to hear your testimony. I want to join my prayers with yours. All of us in this world need to convert ourselves into wanting the mercy of God. Let us not grow weary of aiding his Catholic Church which is criticized constantly in this world.

Celia

Invitation

You might have noticed that God has given many blessings through this message. If Gloria's testimony has been a blessing to you, send us an e-mail with your testimony to info@anewevangelization.com; tell us how this message has helped you, so that we may share it. You can also mail it to us at Mission 2000 P.O. BOX 51986 Phoenix, AZ 85076

Get together with other brothers and sisters and sisters to help us promote this book called "*Standing*

Before God: The Judgment" you can be the medium through which others get closer to Jesus.

Help our mission and tell your friends and family by soliciting this testimony at (480) 234-6106 in Phoenix, AZ, or visit us at www.gloriapolo.us

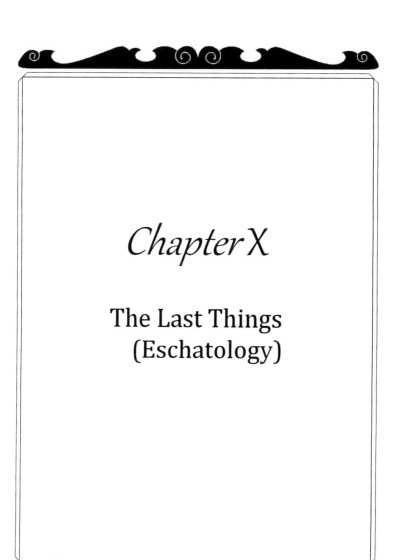

Chapter X

The Last Things
(Eschatology)

Surely, after reading the testimony of Gloria Polo, it has spoken to your heart and now you have a greater hunger to convert and grow in holiness.

At the same time, it is very common for those who read this book to have a hunger to go deeper in these spiritual matters such as death, judgment, heaven, purgatory, and hell (Eschatology).

That is why we have decided to include this section where you will find references to the catechism of the Catholic Church, which is based upon sacred scripture and sacred tradition. It wisely tells us what happens to a man after his death.

This way more people can be ready for their encounter with Jesus Christ, our Lord. We have also included some prayers to help you make decisions in your faith.

All of this is necessary because there are not only protestants that don't believe what we teach, there are also some theologians and "Catholics" that don't accept the teachings of the magisterium of the church.

The Bible, the Apostolic tradition and magisterium of the church are the three pillars that will help you to grow deeper within the testimony of Gloria Polo *"Standing Before God: The Judgment."*

Don't forget to read the quotes in your Bible that are mentioned in the Catechism. We have included some of them to help in your comprehension and impulse to be closer to Jesus Christ:

I.   Death and the Particular Judgment

1021 "Death puts an end to human life as the time open to either accepting or rejecting the divine grace manifested in Christ."(590) The New Testament speaks of judgment primarily in its aspect of the final encounter with Christ in his second coming, but also repeatedly affirms that each will be rewarded immediately after death in accordance with his works and faith. The parable of the poor man Lazarus and the words of Christ on the cross to the good thief, as well as other New Testament texts speak of a final destiny of the soul -a destiny which can be different for some and for others".

1022 "Each man receives his eternal retribution in his immortal soul at the very moment of his death, in a particular judgment that refers his life to Christ: either entrance into the blessedness of heaven-through a purification or immediately,-or immediate and everlasting damnation".

2 Tim 1:9-10; Lk 16:22; 23:43; Mt 16:26; 2 Cor 5:8; Phil 1:23; Heb 9:27; 12:23.
Cf. Council of Lyons II (1274): DS 857-858; Council of Florence; DS 1304- 1306; Council of Trent (1563): DS 1820.

Prayer

"I beg you Lord, that when meditating my own death, it helps me to fight for always living in sanctity. That maintaining myself united with you through prayer and the sacraments, I can give testimony of you. Loving and forgiving my brothers and sisters."

II. The Last Judgment

1038 The resurrection of all the dead, "of both the just and the unjust," will precede the Last Judgment. This will be "the hour when all who are in the tombs will hear [the Son of man's] voice and come forth, those who have done good, to the resurrection of life, and those who have done evil, to the resurrection of judgment."

Then Christ will come "in his glory, and all the angels with him .... Before him will be gathered all the nations, and he will separate them one from another as a shepherd separates the sheep from the goats, and he will place the sheep at his right hand, but the goats at the left.... and they will go away into eternal punishment, but the righteous into eternal life."

1039 In the presence of Christ, who is Truth itself, the truth of each man's relationship with God will be laid bare. The Last Judgment will reveal even to its furthest consequences the good each person has done or failed to do during his earthly life:

All that the wicked do is recorded, and they do not know. When "our God comes, he does not keep silence.". . . he will turn towards those at his left hand:

. . . "I placed my poor little ones on earth for you. I as their head was seated in heaven at the right hand of my Father - but on earth my members were suffering, my members on earth were in need. If you gave anything to my members, what you gave would reach their Head. Would that you had known that my little ones were in need when I placed them on earth for you and appointed them your stewards to bring your good works into my treasury. But you have placed nothing in their hands; therefore you have found nothing in my presence."

1040 The Last Judgment will come when Christ returns in glory. Only the Father knows the day and the hour; only he determines the moment of its coming. Then through his Son Jesus Christ he will pronounce the final word on all history. We shall know the ultimate meaning of the whole work of creation and of the entire economy of salvation and understand the marvellous ways by which his Providence led everything towards its final end. the Last Judgment will reveal that God's justice triumphs over all the injustices committed by his creatures and that God's love is stronger than death.

1041 The message of the Last Judgment calls men to conversion while God is still giving them "the acceptable time, . . . the day of salvation." It inspires a holy fear of God and commits them to the justice of the Kingdom of God. It proclaims the "blessed hope" of the Lord's return, when he will come "to be glorified in his saints, and to be marvelled at in all who have believed.
Acts 24:15; Jn 5:28-29; Mt 25:31; Jn 12:49; Ps 50:3; Song 8:6 2 Cor 6:2 Titus 2:13; 2 Thess 1:10

Prayer

"Lord of Mercy. I love you and ask that you grant me the grace of living in joy, awaiting the holy moment when I can place myself in your hands for judgment. I trust in your mercy so as to be moved by love and not fear, to follow day by day your commandments. Grant me the courage to live like an authentic Christian, so that when the moment comes I may present myself to you with my hands bearing many spiritual fruits, like the Blessed Virgin Mary."

III.   Heaven

1023 Those who die in God's grace and friendship and are perfectly purified live forever with Christ. They are like God for ever, for they "see him as he is," face to face:

By virtue of our apostolic authority, we define the following: According to the general disposition of God, the souls of all the saints . . . and other faithful who died after receiving Christ's holy Baptism (provided they were not in need of purification when they died, . . . or, if they then did need or will need some purification, when they have been purified after death, . . .) already before they take up their bodies again and before the general judgment - and this since the Ascension of our Lord and Savior Jesus Christ into heaven - have been, are and will be in heaven, in the heavenly Kingdom and celestial paradise with Christ, joined to the company of the holy angels. Since the Passion and death of our Lord Jesus Christ, these souls have seen and do see the divine essence with an intuitive vision, and even face to face, without the mediation of any creature.

1024 This perfect life with the Most Holy Trinity - this communion of life and love with the Trinity, with the Virgin Mary, the angels and all the blessed - is called "heaven." Heaven is the ultimate end and fulfillment of the deepest human longings, the state of supreme, definitive happiness.

1025 To live in heaven is "to be with Christ." the elect live "in Christ," but they retain, or rather find, their true identity, their own name.
For life is to be with Christ; where Christ is, there is life, there is the kingdom.

1026 By his death and Resurrection, Jesus Christ has "opened" heaven to us. the life of the blessed consists in the full and perfect possession of the fruits of the redemption accomplished by Christ. He makes partners in his heavenly glorification those who have believed in him and remained faithful to his will. Heaven is the blessed community of all who are perfectly incorporated into Christ.

1027 This mystery of blessed communion with God and all who are in Christ is beyond all understanding and description. Scripture speaks of it in images: life, light, peace, wedding feast, wine of the kingdom, the Father's house, the heavenly Jerusalem, paradise: "no eye has seen, nor ear heard, nor the heart of man conceived, what God has prepared for those who love him."

1028 Because of his transcendence, God cannot be seen as he is, unless he himself opens up his mystery to man's immediate contemplation and gives him the capacity for it. The Church calls this contemplation of God in his heavenly glory "the beatific vision":

How great will your glory and happiness be, to be allowed to see God, to be honored with sharing the joy of salvation and eternal light with Christ your Lord and God... to delight in the joy of immortality in the Kingdom of heaven with the righteous and God's friends.

1029 In the glory of heaven the blessed continue joyfully to fulfill God's will in relation to other men and to all creation. Already they reign with Christ; with him "they shall reign for ever and ever.
1 Jn 3:2 1 Cor 13:12; Rev 22:4; Phil 1:23; Jn 14:3; 1 Thess 4:17; Rev 2:17; 1 Cor 2:9; Rev 22:5; Mt 25:21

*Note: There will not be a paradise on earth like the Jehovah's witnesses claim. We have seen through the Bible and through 2000 years of history that heaven is to be next to God. It will be so beautiful and marvelous, which is why the Bible uses symbols to speak about it.

Prayer
"*Holy Lord. How wonderful is the moment when I can finally become united with you and be fulfilled forever! Our names are written in the book of life, we ask that by your saving grace, our acts of faith, and*

obedience, we can persevere through the end to enjoy your glory forever, Amen."

IV.   The Final Purification, or Purgatory

1030 All who die in God's grace and friendship, but still imperfectly purified, are indeed assured of their eternal salvation; but after death they undergo purification, so as to achieve the holiness necessary to enter the joy of heaven.

1031 The Church gives the name Purgatory to this final purification of the elect, which is entirely different from the punishment of the damned. The Church formulated her doctrine of faith on Purgatory especially at the Councils of Florence and Trent. the tradition of the Church, by reference to certain texts of Scripture, speaks of a cleansing fire.

As for certain lesser faults, we must believe that, before the Final Judgment, there is a purifying fire. He who is truth says that whoever utters blasphemy against the Holy Spirit will be pardoned neither in this age nor in the age to come. From this sentence we understand that certain offenses can be forgiven in this age, but certain others in the age to come.

1032 This teaching is also based on the practice of prayer for the dead, already mentioned in Sacred Scripture: "Therefore Judas Maccabeus] made atonement for the dead, that they might be delivered from their sin." From the beginning the Church has honored the memory of the dead and offered prayers in suffrage for them, above all the Eucharistic sacrifice, so that, thus purified, they may attain the beatific vision of God. The Church also commends almsgiving, indulgences, and works of penance undertaken on behalf of the dead:

Let us help and commemorate them. If Job's sons were purified by their father's sacrifice, why would we doubt that our offerings for the dead bring them some consolation? Let us not hesitate to help those who have died and to offer our prayers for them.
1 Cor 3:15; 1 Pet 1:7; St. Gregory the Great, Dial. 4, 39: PL 77, 396; cf. Mt 12:31; 2 Macc 12:46; Cf. Council of Lyons II (1274): DS 856. St. John Chrysostom, Hom. in 1 Cor. 41, 5: PG 61, 361; cf. Job 1:5.

Prayer
Dear Lord. We love you, but we have also failed you, because we do not do the good that we want, but the evil that we don't. That is why, today I beg you, for all of the holy souls in purgatory and for myself, that at the end of the road, we may pass through the purification. Soon I can enjoy the fullness of your grace in your kingdom, in accompaniment of the Saints and especially of your Holy Mother, The Virgin Mary. Amen!

V.   Hell

1033 We cannot be united with God unless we freely choose to love him. But we cannot love God if we sin gravely against him, against our neighbor or against ourselves: "He who does not love remains in death. Anyone who hates his brother is a murderer, and you know that no murderer has eternal life abiding in him." Our Lord warns us that we shall be separated from him if we fail to meet the serious needs of the poor and the little ones who are his brethren. To die in mortal sin without repenting and accepting God's merciful love means remaining separated from him forever by our own free choice. This state of definitive self-exclusion from communion with God and the blessed is called "hell."

1034 Jesus often speaks of "Gehenna" of "the unquenchable fire" reserved for those who to the end of their lives refuse to believe and be converted, where both soul and body can be lost. Jesus solemnly proclaims that he "will send his angels, and they will gather . . . all evil doers, and throw them into the furnace of fire," and that he will pronounce the condemnation: "Depart from me, you cursed, into the eternal fire!"

1035 The teaching of the Church affirms the existence of hell and its eternity. Immediately after death the souls of those who die in a state of mortal sin descend into hell, where they suffer the punishments of hell, "eternal fire." The chief punishment of hell is eternal separation from God, in whom alone man can possess the life and happiness for which he was created and for which he longs.

1036 The affirmations of Sacred Scripture and the teachings of the Church on the subject of hell are a call to the responsibility incumbent upon man to make use of his freedom in view of his eternal destiny. They are at the same time an urgent call to conversion: "Enter by the narrow gate; for the gate is wide and the way is easy, that leads to destruction, and those who enter by it are many. For the gate is narrow and the way is hard, that leads to life, and those who find it are few."

Since we know neither the day nor the hour, we should follow the advice of the Lord and watch constantly so that, when the single course of our earthly life is completed, we may merit to enter with him into the marriage feast and be numbered among the blessed, and not, like the wicked and slothful servants, be ordered to depart into the eternal fire, into the outer darkness where "men will weep and gnash their teeth."

1037 God predestines no one to go to hell; for this, a willful turning away from God (a mortal sin) is necessary, and persistence in it until the end. In the Eucharistic liturgy and in the daily prayers of her faithful, the Church implores the mercy of God, who does not want "any to perish, but all to come to repentance".

1 Jn 3:14-15; Mt 25:31-46; Mt 5:22; 10:28; Mk 9:43-48; Mt 13:41-42; Mt 25:41; Mt 7:13-14; 2 Pet 3:9.

Prayer

Free me holy Lord of the eternal fire destined for the Devil and his Angels. That I never become ashamed of you, or renounce your love. That I never deny you. It is my wish to never live away from you in suffering. To live in perfect communion with you in your heart.

Amen

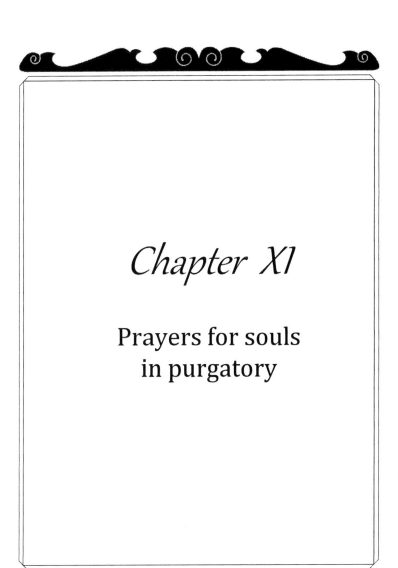

Chapter XI

Prayers for souls
in purgatory

Something that we have to remember in our spiritual lives is to pray for the souls in Purgatory. It wasn't something that the Church invented like Protestants and fundamentalist say, but something that is part of our spiritual life and has been for millennia. Even before those who criticize it even existed. Let us celebrate and pray.

The most famous scriptural reference, among others, concerning these prayers comes from the Old Testament where it is called "*a holy and wholesome thought to pray for the dead, that they may be loosed from sins*" (2 Maccabees 12:46)

Those who attend Mass, pray, and give money to charity or pray for the souls of Purgatory, are working towards their own spiritual well-being. Saint Augustin (Year 450).

We pray for those who were faithful, in this way we remember them and that is how they will remember us. They say that one time they asked St. Augustin, "How much will they pray for me when I died." He answered, "The same amount that you pray for those who have died." The Gospel tells us "In measure that you give, it shall be returned."

"It is Important and necessary to pray for the deceased" Pope John Paul II, (Angelus 2/11/2003)

We pray so that they can be purified in full (1 Cor 3:15-17) That way they can enjoy in perfection the presence of God.

1st. Form

The Prayer of St. Gertrude, below, is one of the most famous of prayers for souls in purgatory. St. Gertrude was a Benedictine nun and mystic who lived in the 13th century.

"Eternal Father, I offer Thee the Most Precious Blood of Thy Divine Son, Jesus, in union with the masses said throughout the world today, for all the holy souls in purgatory, for sinners everywhere, for sinners in the universal church, those in my own home and within my family. Amen".

2nd. Form

"O Lord, who art ever merciful and bounteous with Thy gifts, look down upon the suffering souls in purgatory. Remember not their offenses and negligences, but be mindful of Thy loving mercy, which is from all eternity. Cleanse them of their sins and fulfill their ardent desires that they may be made worthy to behold Thee face to face in Thy glory. May they soon be united with Thee and hear those blessed words which will call them to their heavenly home: "Come, blessed of My Father, take possession of the kingdom prepared for you from the foundation of the world."

116

3th. Form

O Loving Jesus, meek Lamb of God, I, a miserable sinner, salute and worship the most Sacred Wound of Your Shoulder on which You bore Your heavy Cross, which so tore Your Flesh and laid bare Your Bones as to inflict on You an anguish greater than any other Wound of Your Most Blessed Body.

I adore You, O Jesus most sorrowful; I praise and glorify You and give You thanks for this most sacred and painful Wound, beseeching You by the crushing burden of Your heavy Cross to be merciful to the souls in purgatory and to me, a sinner, to forgive me all my mortal and venial sins, and to lead me on towards Heaven along the Way of Your Cross. Amen.

4th. Form

The prayer of St. Augustine (=430) for his mother, St. Monica, is another important testimony from the early Church about prayer for the dead. He wrote:

"Forgive her too, O Lord, if she trespassed against you in the long years of her life after baptism. Forgive her I beseech, you; do not call her to account. Let your mercy give your judgment an honorable welcome, for your words are true and you have promised mercy to the merciful" (Confessions, Book 9:13).

Appendix

Here we can see part of the clinical page where we can find out about your precarious situation. We can see the date and place where she was hospitalized in the clinic of Saint Peter Claver.

RESUMEN HISTORIA CLINICA

los miembros inferiores el 6 May 95 por lo cual se practica
nuevo lavado y fasciotomias de MMII por parte del
servicio de ortopedia. Presenta deterioro multisistemico con
compromiso del gasto urinario, y falla ventilatoria por lo cual
se decide para manejo de UCI a la Clinica ASSISTIR, en donde
se logra manejar la falla ventilatoria. Reingresa a la Clinica
San Pedro el 9 Mayo 95; se continua con manejo medico
y curacion de sus areas quemadas y de las fasciotomias.
Evoluciona satisfactoriamente con epitelizacion de las quemad-
ras y de las fasciotomias. Persiste lesion hepatica y
lesion muscular y nerviosa de MMII, las cuales deben
evaluarse periodicamente. El 25 Mayo 95 es dada de
alta por CIRUGIA, continuando a cargo del servicio de Rehabilitacion, en donde se encuentra hospitalizada actualmente.

Junio 8 de 1.995 - CLINICA SAN PEDRO CLAVER - REHABILITACION

La paciente presenta como secuela de sus quemaduras eléctricas (rayo) lesion parcial
del nervio ciático en forma bilateral con mayor compromiso del nervio ciático poplíteo
externo (bilateral). Se encuentra en tratamiento intensivo de terapia física; reque-
rirá ortesis cortas bilaterales para la marcha. Se dió incapacidad hasta el 5 de
Julio de 1.995 y las siguientes incapacidades dependerán de su evolución.

DRA MARIA LUCIA MARTINEZ
REG MED JG 484-D.E.

In this picture there is a cut-out from the newspaper. An article about the lightning that had struck her. Also in this picture is the moment when they were taking her away on the stretcher.

tal donde se le prac-
os exámenes de rigor.
Ianuel fue conducido
) de lágrimas y llanto.

buseta llevaba pasajeros por lo
que pidió que "por favor de-
nuncien al conductor que le
ocasionó la muerte al pequeño
Jeferson y heridas al abuelo."

El último corte de la s...
en el suministro de ag...
drá lugar en la autopis...
por calle 144; barrio...
Autopista y sus alrede...

Suba varios apar...
n afectados por...
ras que al sur, e...
Agustín, una ...
o una casa. L...
completamente
y los huecos aum...
...rio.
...director de la O
...ción y atenció
...de Bogotá, O
...Grau, dijo que
...o casi todas la
...d y en varias
...a penetrado l
...es pero asegur
...o se han repo
...mentables.
...o en la capital de
...días que no par
...truenos ya cob...

icas, a la nacional

...ion en el sector, la im-
...de las inversiones
...realizan para alcan-
...iversalización del ser-
...mayoría de sus plan-
...os se orientan a for-
Telecom en detrimen-
...mpresas locales".
...el planteamiento, la
...d de competir les per-
...tener economías de
...además utilizar ade-
...ite su infraestructu-
...y humana.
...de las razones con-
...interiormente, el do-
...hace otras propues-
Ierno nacional, como
...zar las funciones
...s de las reguladoras
...del sector, eliminan-
...ncia del ministro de
...ciones en la junta di-
Telecom y cuando se
...re competencia en el
...nder la del Gobierno
...a dicha entidad.
...te, requieren inter-
...ecta en la "determi-
...as políticas que han
...sector y acceder en
...s de equidad al nue-
...e de apertura y li-
...r".

▼ **Se recupera del rayo**

La odontóloga Gloria Polo, de 33 años, quien fue alcanzada el vier...
horas de la tarde por un rayo en la Universidad Nacional, se encuent...
la sala de cuidados intensivos de Assistir. Su estado de salud es r...

EL ESPECTADOR

...as autoridades inform...

Conclusion

One of the most marvelous qualities of God is his infinite mercy and patience. God finds ways to help us receive his Son Jesus Christ and there is no doubt that this testimony "Standing before God: The judgment" is and will be a great blessing to you and many others.

It doesn't matter what we have done before, if one day we decide to get closer to God and call him and ask for his mercy and salvation then we can receive a new life.

Keep moving forward and remember: "Fight to know, live, celebrate, preach, and defend your faith in order to be a committed Christian.

P.S. If this book has helped and blessed you then recommend it to your friends and family. Call us to buy gifts for them and help others to find their way through this testimony.

BOOKS - CD'S - DVDS

To get to know, live, celebrate, preach, and defend the faith, I recommend the following material which is an excellent way to achieve it:

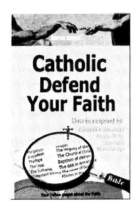

Book
Catholic Defend
Your Faith

In this book you will find a biblical and direct answer for the attacks of the Protestants and fundamentalist sects.

It's a Bestseller that you shouldn't pass up.

Author: Martin Zavala

DVD/CD Standing Before God: The Judgment

Testimony of Gloria Polo

This DVD/CD contains the astonishing testimony of Gloria, who was struck by lightning. God allowed her to see her judgment and now she goes around the world sharing her message.

Book

**I am Catholic,
   So What**

A message that has transformed the lives of thousands by giving them the necessary steps in order to stop being a part of the group of "the crowd" and become a committed Christian.

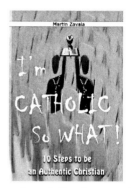

In this book you will discover great spiritual secrets which will drive you towards the life of abundance that God wants for you.

10 Steps to be an Authentic Christian

Excellent to live the New Evangelization

124

You can order this material and others from
Mission 2000

In your nearest bookstore or by contacting us at:

Tel (480) 234-6106
P.O. BOX 51986
PHOENIX, AZ 85076

www.anewevangelization.com

Notes

First Edition: July 2014